# Contents

# Your first rat

Rats can make great pets. They are very intelligent, and they like to play. They also enjoy being with people, so you will need to spend a lot of time with your pet.

But rats are not toys. They are very small and fragile, and easily hurt. You should always be very gentle when handling them.

▲ Rats love to play.

▲ Rats can be very friendly.

# You and Your Pet
# Rat

Jean Coppendale

QED Publishing

Copyright © QED Publishing 2004

First published in the UK in 2004 by
QED Publishing
A Quarto Group Company
226 City Road
London, EC1V 2TT

www.qed-publishing.co.uk

A Catalogue record for this book is available from the British Library.

ISBN 1 84538 287 0

Written by Jean Coppendale
Consultant Michaela Miller
Designed by Susi Martin
Editor Gill Munton
All photographs by Jane Burton except
Page 6 (bottom and top right) and page 7 (centre) by Sue Brown, Pendragon Rattery
Photographs of fruit and vegetables by Chris Taylor
With many thanks to Tanisha Blake and Luke Stent
Picture of Smudge on page 29 by Georgie Meek
Creative Director Louise Morley
Editorial Manager Jean Coppendale

Printed and bound in China

Words in **bold** are
explained on page 32.

**Rats can be easily frightened, especially when they come to a new home.**

**Parent Points**

Rats should be handled carefully and children must always be supervised with their pet rats. If your rat is accidentally dropped, it may break its back or other bones.

Looking after an animal is your responsibility, not your child's. Try to ensure that your child isn't going to become bored with the new pet before you buy one.

Rats are small and you must be gentle with them

**Rats have poor eyesight, so do not make any sudden movements near your pet as this will scare it.**

5

# Lots of rats

All rats have the same shape but they have different markings and colours. Rats which have been bred to be certain colours or mixes of colours are called **fancy rats**.

▶ **Topaz-capped Dumbo rat**

▶ **Ruby-eyed white rat**

▼ **Topaz rat**

**▼ American Blue Dumbo rat**

**► Brown Agouti rat**

**► A black and white Berkshire rat**

# Which rat?

Rats like company, so it is best to buy two rats together. Do not mix rats and mice.

◀ It is best to keep two female or two male rats as pets. If they are from the same litter they are less likely to fight.

▲ **A healthy rat will have a shiny coat and no lumps or rashes on its skin.**

**Parent Points**
When buying rats, ask your vet to recommend reputable breeders or rescue centres in your area. Any rats you buy should come from an environment where they have been handled and cared for properly. Make sure the rat looks bright and inquisitive, and has a clean face and sleek, glossy fur. Check that it is friendly and doesn't bite.

Do not keep female and male rats together as they will have lots of babies which are difficult to look after and find homes for.

▶ **When choosing a pet rat, look for glossy fur and a bright, inquisitive nature.**

◀ **Your rat should have bright, clear eyes and a clean face.**

# Rat shopping list

**Your rat will need:**

▲ **A tank or**
▼ **a cage to live in**

▲ Wood shavings (not cedar or pine) and hay from a pet shop.

# Your rat will need a cosy bed.

▶ **A water bottle**

◀ **Bedding material**

◀ **A carrying box for trips to the vet**

▶ **Rat food**

▶ **A food bowl**

▲ **A scoop for cleaning out the tank**

# Getting ready

The best home for your rat is a glass tank, or aquarium. Make sure that the tank is big enough. It should have a strong lid that your rat cannot push off.

If you choose a cage, make sure that the rat cannot squeeze out between the bars.

If you buy an aquarium to house your rat, do not use an aquarium lid as they do not let in enough air. Ask at a pet shop for a suitable lid for your tank.

▲ **Cover the bottom of the tank or cage with a layer of wood shavings.**

Your pet will need a little nest to sleep in. Buy one from a pet shop, or make one from a small cardboard box. Fill it with special bedding material from a pet shop. Do not use newspaper.

**Parent Points**

The tank or cage should measure at least 60cm x 40cm x 40cm – high enough for the rat to be able to stand up on its hind legs. Make sure that the tank is placed away from draughts, as well as direct sunlight, radiators and other forms of heating. It should not be placed on the floor, or higher than eye level. It should not have a wire floor.

Do not use wood shavings made from cedar or pine in the tank or cage. These can be dangerous to rats.

◀ **You can tear up kitchen towel for your rat's bed**

▲ **Attach the water bottle firmly to the cage.**

# Saying hello

When your rat arrives, it may be feeling very scared. Place it gently in its tank or cage, and leave it alone for a little while to get used to its new home.

After a couple of hours, offer your rat a treat such as a dog biscuit or a small shredded wheat. Hold your hand steady, and wait for your pet to take it from you. Say its name softly as you feed it, so that it begins to know your voice.

▲ **Leave your rat alone if it is sleeping. If it is woken up suddenly, it may become frightened.**

If you have a cage, do not feed your rat through the bars. It will think that anything that comes through the bars – including fingers – can be eaten!

▲ **Keep your hand still when you feed your pet.**

**Parent Points**
Make sure your child knows how to handle the rat before he or she tries to pick it up (see pages 16 and 17).

# Handle with care

To pick up your rat, put one hand on its back and scoop it up with the other hand. Never pick up your rat by its tail. Always sit down when you are holding or playing with your rat. It will like being held against your body but do not squeeze your rat.

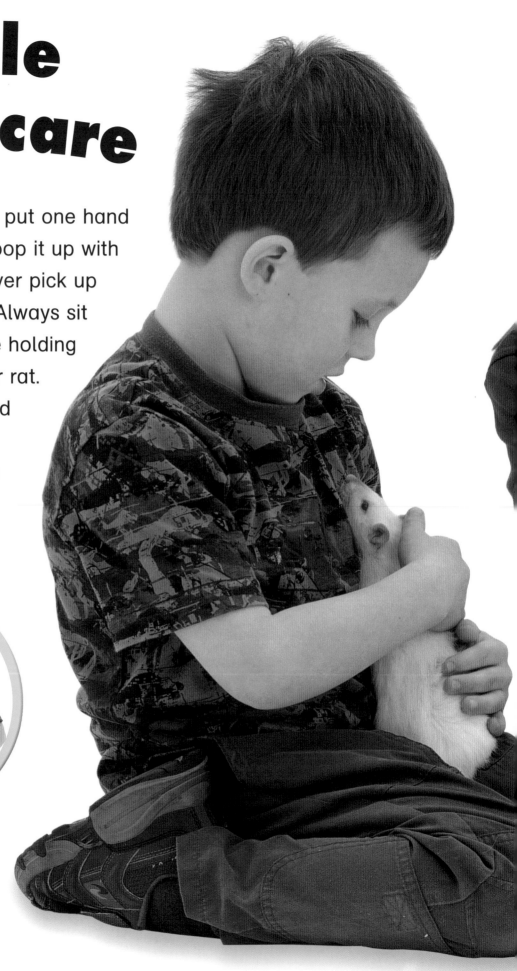

▲ **Stroke your rat gently, from its head to its tail.**

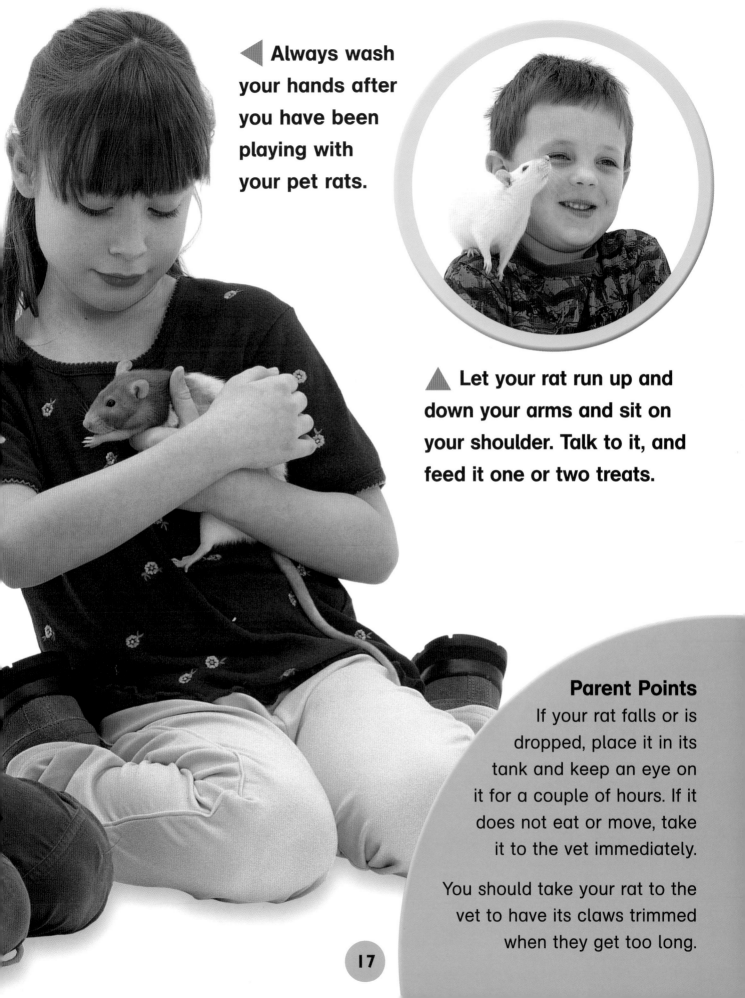

◀ Always wash your hands after you have been playing with your pet rats.

▲ Let your rat run up and down your arms and sit on your shoulder. Talk to it, and feed it one or two treats.

**Parent Points**

If your rat falls or is dropped, place it in its tank and keep an eye on it for a couple of hours. If it does not eat or move, take it to the vet immediately.

You should take your rat to the vet to have its claws trimmed when they get too long.

# Feeding your rat

Your rat should always have food in its bowl. Buy special rat food from a pet shop or from your local vet.

Your rat should have fresh fruit or vegetables every other day. Feed it raw broccoli, corn on the cob, apple, carrot, tomato and celery.

▼ **Apple**

▶ **Carrot**

**Parent Points**

Rats should not be given citrus fruit, pineapple or onion, chicken bones, chocolate, sugary foods or junk food.

Children should never be allowed to tease pets with food, or offer food and then snatch it away.

▲ **Rats like lots of different foods to nibble.**

Your rat will love a treat every now and then. Try puffed wheat or buy some rat chews from a pet shop.

It is good for your rat to have different foods to eat. Try feeding it some leftovers such as pasta, wholemeal bread or cooked potato. Give it a bone to chew – this will be tasty and will help to keep its teeth healthy. But never give your pet chicken bones as they will make it choke.

▶ **Broccoli**

▼ **Celery**

▶ **Pasta**

▲ **Baby corn**

# Keep it clean

Your rat's home needs to be kept clean. Once a day, use a scoop to clear out any old bits of food. Your rat will probably have a toilet corner in the tank, and this should be cleaned out every day.

Once a week, replace the old wood shavings and bedding.

▲ **Scoop out the dirty wood shavings from your rat's tank every day.**

While you are cleaning out the cage, put your rat somewhere safe. Have a special box with some bedding and air holes in the lid. Do not leave your pet in here for very long or it will get scared.

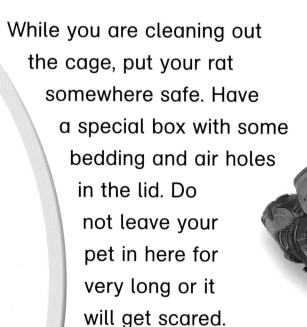

▶ **Wash your rat's food bowl each day.**

◀ **Clean your pet's water bottle with a bottle brush once a week.**

The tank and all your rat's toys should be washed with a little disinfectant about once a week. Always wash your hands after cleaning out the tank.

**Parent Points**
Use animal-safe disinfectant (available from pet shops) for cleaning the tank. Make sure your rat is put somewhere safe while its home is being cleaned.

21

# Your rat's life cycle

A female rat is ready to have babies when she is about 8 weeks old.

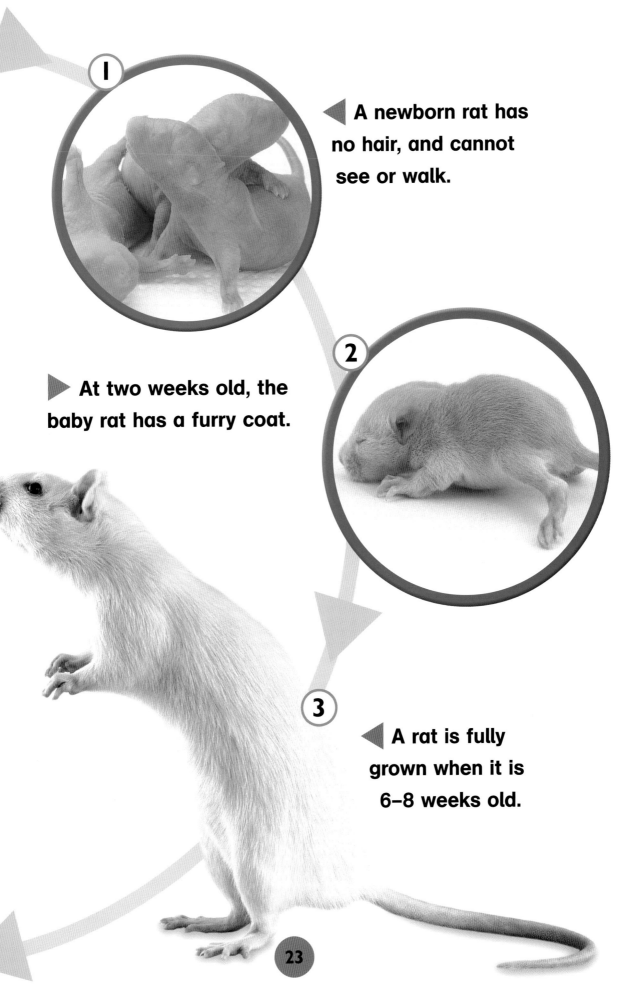

**◀ A newborn rat has no hair, and cannot see or walk.**

**▶ At two weeks old, the baby rat has a furry coat.**

**◀ A rat is fully grown when it is 6–8 weeks old.**

# Let's play!

◀ **Have fun making a play area for your rat**

▲ **Rats love to explore**

Rats love to play. Place some play bricks on the floor so that your pet can run between them. Give it a small ball to play with.

Place some boxes, baskets, cardboard tubes or paper bags on the floor for your pet to climb in and out of.

**▲ Rats are good climbers**

Rats love to climb and have a good sense of balance. Give them bird perches, ropes and ladders to play on.

# Make a rat playground

Make a playground of coloured bricks, toys, cardboard tubes and ladders for your pets. Make sure that nothing will topple over and hurt your pets.

# Saying goodbye

As your rat grows older, it will play less and spend more time sleeping. If your rat is very old or ill, it may need to be put to sleep or it may die in its sleep.
Try not to be too sad, and remember all the fun you had together.

You may want to bury your pet in the garden, but you can take it to the vet if you prefer.

Smudge last summer

◀ **If your rat is not breathing properly or cannot eat, you should take it to the vet.**

My rat Smudge

Remember all the fun you had together

# Rat checklist

Read this list, and think about all the points.

✔ Rats are not toys.

✔ How will you treat your rat if it makes you angry?

✔ Animals feel pain, just as you do.

✔ Treat your rat gently – as you would like to be treated yourself.

✔ Most rats live for about two to three years – will you get bored with your pet?

✔ Will you be happy to clean out your pet's tank every day?

✔ Never hit your rat, shout at it, drop it or throw things at it.

# Parents' checklist

● You, not your child, are responsible for the care of your pet rat.

● Rats are very sociable and need lots of company. Do you and your family have enough time for these pets?

● Rats are very intelligent and can be trained, but this takes time and patience.

● Your rat will need someone to look after it when you are away from home.

● A rat will only bite if it is teased with food, if it mistakes fingers for food or if it is scared or angry.

● A rat is a small pet and can easily be stepped on – make sure your child is aware of the dangers.

● Always supervise pets and children.

# Rat words

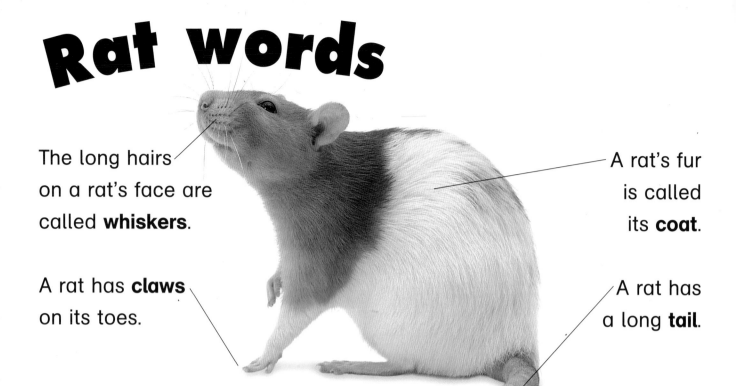

The long hairs on a rat's face are called **whiskers**.

A rat's fur is called its **coat**.

A rat has **claws** on its toes.

A rat has a long **tail**.

**Fancy rats** Rats which have been bred to be particular mixes of colours are called fancy rats. Some fancy rats have been bred to have special features such as big ears.

**Litter** A group of young produced at the same time by a mammal

# Index